SPIRITUAL

SUCCESS

Developing

Your Own

Daily Practice

SPIRITUAL

SUCCESS

Developing

Your Own

Daily Practice

Ruth L. Miller

SPIRITBOOKS

Spiritual Success: developing your own
daily practice

Published by
SPIRITBOOKS
 An imprint of: Portal Center Press
Oregon, USA

www.portalcenterpress.com

ISBN: 978-1-936902-41-5

Contents

Introduction

Throughout time and around the world, all of humanity has sought a way of life that moves beyond maintaining a healthy body, home, and family. They've looked for ways to discover and maintain a connection with the source of life, power, and intelligence.

Even the most ancient humans, living in the most primitive circumstances, knew that life was something separate from the body—they watched it come and go. They could feel knowledge that came from other than the five senses: inspiration and what we call "extrasensory perception." They watched healing happen and people could feel a special kind of power moving through their bodies. They could see that the most successful people among them were able to "tap into" this awareness and power, and they wanted to do the same.

Each religion was created to provide a way for many people in a culture to do this. Religions evolved to fit the cultural context in which they were born, so they have different terms and processes. They acknowledged that different people had different levels of skill and different ways of under-standing and so provided different roles and training.

They all, however, have one purpose: to encourage and support a balance of spiritual, physical, and social activity in each person's life so as to maximize their comfort, peace, and security.

If we look at the various religious practices around the world and across time from this point of view, we find a number of commonalities:

- Regular study of inspiring[1] texts (or listening to inspired speakers);
- Regular contemplation of inspiring ideas;
- Regular expansion of the sense of self into a sense of connection or union with something larger;
- Training and discipline to enhance our ability to do the above or provide it for others;

---

[1] "Inspiring" literally means "in-spirit-ing." *Spirit* comes from a Latin word that means both "spirit" and "breath" So respiration is as much about taking in spirit as about air, and to expire (an out-of-style English word for die) is "spirit-from" or to let go of spirit.

- Occasional changes in patterns of physical and social activity (holy days);
- Frequent (at least weekly) gatherings with others doing similar things and thinking in similar ways.

Early religious practices used the power of natural forces to help people get in touch with the "Something Greater" that is the source of our life and inspiration. We now call these, "earth-centered" religions. Most of them involve the whole community in daily, monthly, and seasonal variations of these practices that help strengthen the community as well as the individual's capacity to feel and work with the power of life and the intelligence that extends beyond sens-ory input. All of them have practices for individuals that depend on that person's interest in and capacity for tapping into this awareness and power.

At some point along the way, as tribal groups begin to gather into urban centers, there is a shift. When city walls are built, earth's power is not so immediate, so other metaphors are used to help people shift their focus away from their physical and social lives. In most cases, one or two historical figures are held up as models of perfection, having all the power and wisdom and life that anybody can imagine. By focusing on them, people hope to bring those attributes into themselves and begin to live a more complete and balanced life.

European historians and anthropologists, with their own cultural perspectives and preconceptions, have typically called these figures "gods" and "goddesses," and they've taught the people they were studying that these are the English words for the images and ideals those people venerate. But in most cases, if one goes behind the outer forms, one finds that the forms mean little to the people who make them.

The essential teaching is that there is one unnamable and unknowable source of life, wisdom, and power that underlies all human experience and everyone has the capacity to "tap into" it. All other names, forms, and ideas are understood as simply ways to get people there.

For "people of the book"—Jews, Muslims, and Christians—that one power, life, and wisdom is called God in English, *Al'Lah* in Arabic. For people raised on the *Vedas*— Hindus, Jains, Buddhists, and Sikhs—that underlying life, wisdom and power is *Brahman.* For many Chinese, it is *Tao.* Among the first peoples of North America, it is now known as Great Spirit. Among the ancient Egyptians it was *Neter;* the ancient Greeks called it *Theos;* the Romans called it *Deus;* people in the 12-step movement call it their "Higher Power." And for all of them, the goal of every practice is to break down any barriers between our normal waking awareness and our awareness of that life, wisdom, and power working in us, around us, and through us.

This guide aims to do the same. It takes the common elements listed above and provides a series of practices and processes that help build a balanced life. While they're provided outside of any particular religious context, they are totally adaptable to fit whatever religion the practitioner feels at home in. As the 14th Dalai Lama, the last head of the Tibetan religion and government (now in exile), has said so often: "stay within your own religious heritage... stick to your roots... do the practice."

Practice One: Study

Regardless of what we know, or think we know; no matter how many times we have felt that delicious state of union that all religious practices are designed to guide us toward, the intellect needs to be "re-minded" of the fundamentals.

For this reason, the first step in all spiritual practice is listening to, or reading (or, ideally, both!), the words and ideas of profound thinkers, prophets and mystics who have gone on the path before us. We spend a few minutes each day studying and a few hours one day each week.

What to study? Whatever feeds your soul in the moment—and that will usually depend on your background and inclinations. This section offers some guidelines and suggestions.

Sacred Texts

We've all heard of various sacred texts, on which many people have based their values, morals, and behavior.

- For Christians, the Bible, with its Old and New Testament, is the revealed Word of God, with guidance for every situation.
- For Jews it is *Torah*, provided by God's prophets for the enlightenment of God's own people.
- For Muslims, it is *Qur'an,* the divinely inspired revelation given to the last great prophet, Mohammed (blessed be his name).

- For Hindus and its branches, the ancient *Vedas,* written by many great saints, philosophers, and historians around 5000 years ago, inspire and inform.
- For Buddhists, contemplating the *Sutras* of Gautama and later Buddhas is essential for understanding.
- The *Tao te Ching* and the *I Ching* serve Taoists and many Confucians, along with other writings by other great masters *Lao tse, Kun fu tse* (Confucius) and *Chuang tse.*

And so forth—each great tradition has its sacred text.

These ancient writings—the most recent of which is nearly 1500 years old—have stood the test of time. They have guided countless generations through difficult challenges and wondrous, miraculous events. They have provided insight where there had been confusion, options where there had been and impasse, authoritative counsel where there had been ignorance and misunderstanding.

In addition to these basic texts, each tradition has many, even thousands of, commentaries—some of which have taken on even more importance in daily life than the original sacred text. Most of these commentaries were written centuries ago by people who built their lives around understanding the texts and applying them to the problems of the time and culture in which they lived. Some of them apply equally well today.

Today, we have new commentaries on the ancient texts—and new ancient texts! The Dead Sea Scrolls and the Nag Hammadi library have provided a wealth of new sources of inspiration, including:

- The Gospel of Thomas
- The Gospel of Philip
- The Isaiah Scroll
- "New" Apocrypha
- "New" Infancy gospels
- "New" letters by apostles

and many others. Many of these may be found in the collection entitled *The Other Bible* compiled by Willis Barnstone.

In addition to these larger volumes, most spiritual traditions—and denominations within those traditions—publish daily guides with sacred readings, commentaries, and a word or phrase to consider through the day. *The Daily Word* is among the oldest of these.

Interpretations of Other Traditions

As the boundaries of our world have dissolved, various students and scholars have interpreted one culture's religious practices and principles in terms that others can understand. Perhaps the foremost of these are:

- Alan Watts, *Nature, Man, and Woman;* and *The Book on the Taboo Against Knowing Who You Are;*
- Christopher Isherwood & Pravananda, *How to Know God, the yoga aphorisms of Patanjali.*
- Joseph Campbell, *The Hero's Journey;* and *The Masks of God;*
- Ram Dass, *The Only Dance There Is;*
- Matthew Fox, *Original Blessing;* and *Natural Grace;*
- Max Freedom Long, *The Secret Science at Work;*

- David Abrams, *The Spell of the Sensuous;*
- Michael Harner, *The Way of the Shaman;*
- Thich Nhat Hanh, *Living Buddha, Living Christ.*

Modern Revelations

We also have new revelations—some of which are based on and use the language of previous texts, and some of which seem specific to the culture and time in which we live. Among these are

- *A Course in Miracles*, in which the narrator, who identifies himself as Jesus Christ, provides pages and pages of instruction on how to eliminate the barrier between normal awareness (ego) and conscious communion with the Father through Him.

15

- *Conversations with God,* in which a man who has reached "rock bottom" finally allows himself to hear (and write down) what the Voice of God has been saying to him all along.
- *Vision* and related books, revealed to a man who has chosen to live close to nature out of concern for the wellbeing of all life.
- *Emanuel's Book,* in which many questions about daily life, the universe, and the after-life are answered by a woman's "Higher Self."

And many others. The loving guidance to be found in these texts parallels that of many traditional texts, and, because they're addressed to people in the modern world, often seem more relevant.

Their ever-evolving understandings of the universe and the mind are leading many scientists to provide useful texts, as well. Among them are:

- psychologist Wayne Dyer's interpretations of our relationship with ourselves and our world;
- physicist Amit Goswami's interpretations of quantum consciousness;
- endocrinologist Deepak Chopra's interpretations of the relationship between mind and body;
- computer scientists Gregg Braden's interpretations of the prayerful nature of various codes in our language and our bodies;
- physicist/philosopher Dana Zohar's analyses of the nature of relationship based on quantum mechanics.
- psychiatrist Brian Weiss' explorations of his clients' "other lifetimes;"

- molecular biologist Bruce Lipton's interpretation of how the cell develops in direct response to our thoughts and feelings;
- biochemist Masuro Emoto's descriptions (and photographs!) of water's response to words, music, and prayer.

Applied Principles

Then there are the works of those who, intentionally or unwittingly, have learned to work with the higher power to facilitate the healing process in the minds and bodies of those around them, most notably:

- Louise Hay's *You Can Heal Your Life*;
- Carolyn Myss' *Anatomy of the Spirit;*

- Joel Goldsmith's *Spiritual Healing;* and *Conscious Union with God;*
- Mary Baker Eddy's *Science & Health with Key to the Scriptures;*
- Charles Fillmore's *Christian Healing;*
- Ernest Holmes' *Science of Mind;*
- Ron Roth's *Healing Path of Prayer.*

There are also those who, seeing life's challenges, have found ways to apply ancient principles and practices in the modern context. A few of these are:

- *Spiritual Economics* by Eric Butterworth
- *Peace of Mind* by Joshua Loth Liebman
- *Grow Rich with Peace of Mind* by Napoleon Hill
- *The Game of Life and How to Play it* by Florence Scovell Shinn

- *This Thing Called You* by Ernest Holmes.

And, from earlier thinkers,
- The essays of Ralph Waldo Emerson[2]
- The poetry of Whitman, Goethe, and other transcendentalists
- *High Mysticism*, *The Gospel Series* and others by Emma Curtis Hopkins[3]

Fiction

Finally, there are wonderful imaginary adventures that have been written down for us to see what it

---

[2] If you feel intimidated by Emerson's Victorian prose, try Miller's modernization of his primary texts, called *Natural Abundance*, published by Beyond Words/Simon & Schuster.

[3] Miller has "translated" Hopkins' often-difficult stream of consciousness lectures and delineated her suggestions for daily practice in the book *Unveiling Your Hidden Power*, published by WiseWoman Press.

might be like to live in the awareness of our true nature. Some
better-known ones include:

- Richard Bach's *Illusions*
- Joseph Girzione's *Joshua*
- Jane Roberts' *Education of Oversoul Seven*
- James Redfield's *Celestine Prophecy;* and *The Tenth Insight;*
- Zenna Henderson's *The People* and *Pilgrimage: the book of the people;*

All of these texts can be useful
reminders of who we really are and
what our lives can truly become.

NOTE: listening to spiritual
music can be as effective as reading
or listening to speakers as a way to
remind us about our true nature—

and great music can be found to support all religious traditions.[4]

---

[4] If you're not part of a religious community, you can find great quantities of good music online. If you're looking for something to help you focus on the goodness of life, a group called Empower Music & Arts collects and promotes positive spiritual music by contemporary musicians and even offers an online radio station at www.empowerma.com.

Practice Two: Silence

All the world's spiritual and religious traditions include some combination of

- Contemplation
- Prayer
- Meditation

These are different, but not mutually exclusive, activities. They all involve being alone and quiet. They all lead the practitioner out of normal waking "chatter" into a state of consciousness that can effectively "tap into" the Higher Power that fills, surrounds, and enfolds us. And for some people, they are sequential: each activity leads into the next.

Contemplation

Contemplation flows easily from one's study. Having immersed ourselves for some minutes (or hours) in another person's ideas, revelation, or interpretation, we set the text aside, close our eyes, and sit with it.

After a time we may decide to open our eyes, get up, and walk with it. But still this work, this concept or set of concepts, remains the focus of our attention. We play with it, allow connections to form in our minds and follow those connections—always re-turning to the ideas expressed in the text. We consider what the writer was experiencing. We imagine applying the idea in our own lives—in the past, present, or some possible future. We link it to other, similar or contrasting texts, and build a logical bridge between them. We decide whether this idea or set of ideas makes sense to us and if so, why; and if not, why not. In short, we make the text our own.

This process may last a few minutes, hours, or even weeks—depending on how closely related the ideas in the text are to the ideas we already hold.

If, after a few moments' contemplation, the ideas make no sense to you, set them aside to explore with your spiritual teacher, counselor, or director. There may be a missing link in your experience that the more experienced guide can provide to help you understand it.

Another form of contemplation occurs in the presence of beauty or other powerful experience. We often contemplate a piece of art or a beautiful sunset. We may also contemplate a wonderful piece of music or the process of a master (of anything—from carpentry to basketball!) at work. Many religious traditions encourage contemplation of the words in a beloved prayer or hymn. The process is the same:

- Observe the focus-object.
- Consider many aspects of the focus-object.
- Allow connections to form and follow them, returning to the focus.
- Imagine what it was like to produce what you're focusing on.
- Imagine producing or applying the same in your own life—past, present, or some possible future.
- Connect this focus with your other experiences and ideas.

- Build a logical bridge between this and your other experiences and ideas.
- Rest with the new understanding that is emerging in this process.

Prayer

Though it may begin with contemplation, prayer is different from contemplation in several ways. In prayer, we're saying what's on our minds, describing what we are ready to let go of and what we'd like to see more of. In prayer, we're focused, we're seeking, we're intending, we're aiming for a particular outcome.

The practice of prayer is consistent across traditions and around the world:

- Start with a known formula, a familiar set of words or phrases that brings us into awareness of the presence of divine power;

- State specific intentions—experiences and feelings we're ready to be done with and those we're ready to have more of;
- Express gratitude and appreciation that the prayer has been heard;
- Affirm that "it is done" (one meaning of the word *Amen);*

In most traditions there are "outer" (exoteric, or beginner, open to anyone) and "inner" (esoteric, or advanced, limited to those who have studied) teachings around prayer. The Outer teachings stick to the above structure and focus on the formulas. Then, when someone begins to ask questions or seems to sincerely seek a deeper experience, they're introduced to the Inner, or more advanced, teachings.

The more advanced teachings around prayer have to do with the "feeling state" that the praying person achieves. In these teachings, meditation and prayer become closely linked. The goal of the process shifts. From saying the right thing in the right way so it will be heard and acted upon by the divine Power, the focus becomes achieving a state of consciousness. In this new state the praying person *feels* the Presence of the Power and *knows* that whatever intention was focused on in this prayer session is fulfilled.[5]

In most Pentecostal Christian churches and some charismatic Catholic groups, this experience is

---

[5] Miller's *Uncommon Prayer* provides a more complete explanation and set of guidelines for this process.

called "the Anointing." In New Thought[6] churches and centers, it's called "treatment" or "positive prayer."

Prayer, like all spiritual practices, is most effective when done regularly: the occasional "call for help" is not enough to maintain spiritual balance.

The problem with prayer, however, is that it requires a belief in some form of Higher Power—and many modern thinkers have a hard time with that one. They are uncomfortable with the idea of an "Old Man in the sky" and don't have another model to use.

---

[6] New Thought includes Unity, Religious Science, Centers for Spiritual Living, Science of Mind, Divine Science, and Sanctuaries and Homes of Truth (Note: New Thought does *not* include Scientology).

This is where the study of spiritual literature becomes very important. As the introduction to this guide suggests, a comprehensive review of human cultures shows that *all* of humanity honors some power greater than any of us, individually or collectively, simply because of their experience. Too much goes on—from storms to healings to prophetic visions—that cannot be explained by the knowledge and power of the human mind alone.

Meditation

At some point the acts of contemplation and prayer can lead to the activity that has been called meditation.

There's a state of consciousness in which nothing seems to exist in form—and yet everything still, gloriously, *is*. Every culture and spiritual tradition has their own name for this state of being. Christian mystics called it *The Ecstasy*. Hindu *yogis* call it *Samadhi* or *Sat chit ananda* (love-bliss conscious-ness). Some Muslims call it *Rapture*. Many modern mystics simply call it *Home*.

This state of consciousness is achieved through the practice of meditation. It may take years of practice to achieve—or, for some, may be experienced the first time they close their eyes and breathe deeply into the silence along with a group of like-minded folks.

There are two basic approaches in meditation: mind-emptying and mind-filling.

- Mind-emptying practices invite us to withdraw our awareness from the external world into the body and then methodically withdraw our awareness from different parts of the body.[7] Some say to focus all awareness into a place in the brain (usually the "3rd-eye center" a few inches behind the bridge of the nose); others focus on the heart. The final stage is where all is at first dark, then becomes a wonderful light.

- Mind-filling practices use repeated words or phrases, (called

---

[7] This is the essence of "Self-realization" or *Kriya yoga* introduced in the U.S. by Paramahansa Yogananda in the 1920s.

mantras in Hindi)[8] and breathing practices to keep "monkey mind" (our normal thinking mind) occupied until the true Self, with Pure Awareness, can be experienced.

Both of these approaches work. Some work better for some people at some times. And in both processes, the actual achievement of the state happens spontaneously— almost when we're not looking—so "working at it" or striving, is useless. Meditation is a practice that leads to a result that our conscious minds have no control over—in fact occurs when our conscious, waking, thinking minds are shut down.

---

[8] This is the essence of Transcendental Meditation (TM), which was introduced to the U.S. by *Maharishi* Mahesh Yogi.

But even if we don't experience that state, the practice of meditation is useful. It can

- Help us get out of our normal thought processes;
- Relax the body;
- Reduce anxiety;
- Lower blood pressure and improves heart function;
- Harmonize body systems.[9]

Beyond all that, meditation helps us to let go of our attachment to *doing*. It helps us to see that *being* is where our power is. It's why Mohandas K. (*Mahatma*) Gandhi said "We must *be* the change we wish to see in the world."

---

[9] For a more complete description of the methods and benefits of meditation see *Calm Healing* by Robert Bruce Newman and Ruth L Miller (North Atlantic Books, 2006).

Finally, meditation is a practice of "being aware." In some spiritual traditions, it's called "listening."

In meditation, we are not speaking or writing or doing anything. In meditation we are expecting something. We sit (or walk or float or recline) in silence, comfortably relaxed and expecting to become aware of something. That's all.

It's like seeing the maestro's baton go up and knowing that a sound is about to happen—we're expecting it at any moment. Or watching someone step on stage, or to the rostrum or pulpit, and pick up the microphone, holding it in front of their mouth. We *know* we're about to hear something so we wait, comfortably, expecting it.[10]

For most people, the outcome of such a session is a sense of peace and harmony, balance and readiness. For some, the experience resulting from this state is "hearing" the "Voice of God." For some, the outcome is inspired creative energy. For others, it's a vision of possibility or guidance.

Meditation is most effective when it is practiced daily, at least 15 minutes once a day and preferably 20-30 minutes twice a day.

---

[10] In one Christian sect, Unity, this is the accepted interpretation of the Biblical phrase "Waiting upon the Lord."

Practice Three: Sharing

Almost every great spiritual teacher has enjoined his/her followers to "go out and spread the good news." Although this may sound a bit like marketing, it's really a part of the process of learning and of integrating what's being learned.

We've all heard the doctrine, "you teach best that which you need to learn." Or, "those who can't, teach." Teaching others, or sharing what we're discovering, is the best possible way to integrate a new set of ideas, principles, and practices into our own mental framework.

It's also the best way to ensure that one's own practice doesn't become "automatic," "habitual," or "unconscious." When we must describe to another person what works, why it works, and what the results have been for us, we're far less likely to simply do something "by rote" without paying attention to what and how we're doing it.

So the third important way to maintain our own spiritual life and practice is to share our understanding and experience of it with others.

There are three effective ways to share:

- respond to another's need or request;
- "broadcast" to the world (through the media: books, blogs, etc.);

- open our hearts to a few people in letters or quiet conversation.

The other option—imposing our ideas on the people around us, regardless of their readiness to hear or accept—does no good for anyone.

It's easy to get caught up in the excitement of sharing, to start telling the people around us the good news that we've heard and how much better their life would be if they did things the way we're learning to. (Some people call this "new-convert-itis.")

While this kind of enthusiasm is wonderful to behold, most of the people around us are not interested or ready to hear all the ways they "should" do what we're doing. That's not sharing, or even evangelism.

Responding to a request

When we're calm, peaceful, enjoying life, the people around us notice—and usually want "what we've got." Sometimes they'll ask directly what we do and how we do it. Then it's easy. We simply tell them what we've been learning and experiencing. No pressure; no justification; just a relaxed, comfortable "well, lately I've been ... and it's really ... for me." Or words to that effect.

Sometimes, though, they're not able to directly ask. Sometimes they will, instead, set up opportunities for us to "help" them, or will arrange to be around us a lot, hoping to learn "by osmosis." Sometimes they'll start "acting out" in jealousy or envy.

This is still a request—however indirect. Our best choice in both cases is not to get caught up in their issues or behavior, but simply to be and do who and what we know best. They'll either get it or they won't— and they'll either ask for more or move on in time.

Broadcasting

Wanting to tell the world all the good things we've been learning and discovering and experiencing is a normal response. All primates, from birds to elephants to whales and gorillas, announce to the world when they've had a wonderful experience and feel really good about themselves.

Humans do so in far more ways. We write songs, create dances, write books and articles, post things on the internet, produce films and tv or radio programs, run for office, and found schools and churches to tell the world the wonderful new experiences and understandings we're having.

It's normal, and often very effective. The word gets out; people respond; some behaviors change—and the person who started it all gets the extra satisfaction of having shared.

The problem with most of these forms of sharing is that though many people encounter the material over many days, weeks, and often years—the person doing the sharing has done so only once.

So there's a felt need for more sharing. Sometimes this is handled in the marketing and p.r. process—lots of lectures, interviews, follow-up articles, etc. provide more opportunities to build on the original ideas and experiences.

But something happens along the way—new understandings and experiences create new learnings that want to be shared. This is great, but the world usually wants more of the original sharing, not the "new stuff."

So the "broadcaster" has to make a choice: continue to build on the old stuff to maintain a good relationship with the fans, or withdraw and find a way to share the new stuff—and run the risk of losing all the fans and perks that have come from the previous sharing.

The way through this dilemma is to go back and do the other steps for maintaining the Spirit connection:

study, silence, and (as we'll explore in the next chapter) service. When we engage regularly and frequently in those activities, there's no more dilemma; the way becomes clear.

Letters, Journals & Dialogue

The word "dialogue" means "through the word." It's not the same as "discussion," which comes from the same root as "percussion" and "concussion," and so suggests "hitting each other." When two or more people come together in dialogue, they speak and listen from the heart and something entirely new emerges, something that didn't exist in anyone's awareness before. When one person sits down to write to another from the same heart-center, what emerges on paper is

more than that person had ever
thought or felt before.

Sharing of this kind is actually
more than simply sharing—it's a
creative process that extends our
experience and understanding fur-
ther. Simply opening our hearts
when we speak and to listen to
what others have to say is all it
takes.

This is the great power of good
"support groups." In them we listen
with open hearts; we share with
open hearts; all of us experience
more than any of us brought.

Some of the most profoundly
moving literature in the world was
originally written as letters. Over
half the New Testament is letters
(called "epistles," from the Greek).
When we sit down with the
intention of sharing what's in our

heart, and allow the pen (or key-strokes) to flow without censorship, we're often amazed at what comes out. And, if we do so with any regularity, we find that such sharing is a satisfying part of our spiritual practice.

A variation on sharing by means of letters is the use of a journal. Since the Renaissance, and especially through the 18th and 19th centuries, maintaining diaries and journals was an essential part of every educated person's spiritual and emotional life. Ralph Waldo Emerson's journals filled a library. Thomas Jefferson's likewise.

Across those centuries, women and men used journals to express their hearts and minds and to "work out" through the writing process whatever clarity they sought in challenging situations.

In the 1980s the use of journals as an aid to spiritual and emotional development was reintroduced in the U.S. in Ira Progoff's workshops and in books like *The Artist's Way.*

In all these forms, heart-centered expression of one's understandings and experiences enhances the power of both in our lives.

Practice Four: Service

Another consistency across world spiritual traditions is the call to service. At first, the service is to the source of spiritual support and training: the apprentice serves the shaman; the disciple serves the master; the acolyte serves the priest; the monk serves the order. Then, with mastery, the focus of service shifts to the larger community: the apostles are sent into the villages to heal and teach; the abbots set up new houses; the priests set up new churches or temples; the shaman-in-training replaces the elder shaman in service to the community.

Not all of us are called to do that work, but all of us are called to serve. We serve our families by allowing the loving, nurturing presence that we encounter in the silence to guide our actions in greater love and support. We serve our communities by joyfully sharing the gifts and talents we were born with or have developed in love and peace. We serve humanity by recognizing that, in spirit, at the core, we are all One.

Expressing Our Gifts

In its finest form, service is using the gifts we were born with in a way that gives joy, delight, and a fuller experience of love, light, and wisdom to those around us—as they increase our own.

Our gifts may include a wide variety of possibilities. They usually fall within some set of seven basic categories, or "intelligences:"

- Visual (capacity to see and/or create visual patterns, colors, scenes)
- Musical/mathematical (capacity to comprehend and/or generate complex relationships)
- Spatial (capacity to perceive where things are in relation to each other & create harmonious patterns)
- Movement/kinesthetic (body-awareness; athleticism; capacity to translate other forms into movement)
- Interpersonal (capacity to perceive, express, and fulfill needs and desires of others)

- Intrapersonal (capacity to monitor inner processes, imagine, express deep, inner feelings)
- Mechanical (capacity to comprehend and/or create interacting movements of objects)

Some of us see and express ourselves to others well through images or words. Some of us experience and express ourselves well through the patterns of relationships in music or math (the movie *August Rush* being the ultimate example of this ability!). Some of us are very good at "reading" others and addressing their needs. Others are more skilled at going inside and understanding emotions or thought processes. The visual/kinesthetic person will dance beautifully. The mechanical/spatial person will create fabulous buildings, sculptures, and vehicles. And so forth.

All of us are skilled in several of these areas.

So we can play music or play games or write books or push wheelchairs—all in the name of service. We can cook a meal or clean up after one, restoring order and beauty. We can perform a dance or provide a space for someone else to do so. We can teach children or recycle trash or plant a garden or write a check or hold someone's hand—whatever is our joy to offer in the moment.

To truly serve is to act in the most delightful, satisfying way for us and those around us to express our gifts and skills for the betterment of our world.

To serve is *not* to sacrifice oneself for the sake of others: "self-sacrifice leaves no one to get the job done." We can't hope to be effective if we drain ourselves: our cup *must* "runneth over" if we are to truly be of service.

Effective service *always* involves the "3 Es:" our actions are Effortless, Energizing, and Enjoyable. They're effortless in that we don't have to "make ourselves" do it. They're energizing in the very doing, so when we're done we feel as good as, or even better than, we felt before we started. They're enjoyable, because we're being and doing what we love to be and do!

It works this way because we're allowing our true essence to be expressed and experienced, and so we're "obeying" our essential nature. Actions that are forced, pressured, hurried, draining are *never* as effective—and often do more harm than good in our world.

Service is essential to maintaining our spirits because it's the means by which the inner experiences are ex-pressed and reinforced in the world around us. The world responds in turn, and we are expanded in the process.

Responding to Requests for Aid

Most of us have been trained to believe that we're not serving others unless they "need" us. We were told that service is about doing for others. So, when we feel the call to serve, we look for people or organizations who are asking for something that we're willing to give. We try to make sure that what we're being asked to do is really "good for them" and we do our best to meet those needs.

In most cases, this kind of effort is wasted. Sad but true. People and organizations who are asking for "help" are almost always really saying they've lost sight of their inner source of inspiration and support. They've turned to the outside world, forgetting that the outer world can't begin to give us what we need—only the inner world can.

For example, the man seeking a "hand-out" is usually saying: "I've given up on myself and forgotten that I have gifts to give." The abused mother seeking shelter is too often saying: "I gave away my power so many times I don't even know how to find it any more." The nonprofit organization seeking donations is often saying "we don't trust that the work we do will support itself so we're looking for others to reassure us."

So, unless we're skilled at reminding others where their true source of support is and how to find it, we're usually "enabling" their continued distress rather than truly serving them with our aid.

Knowing When and How

This means that often our best acts of service are more like "random acts of kindness and senseless beauty" than "rescuing damsels in distress."

When can we best serve? We find out by checking inside: We check to see how our body feels when we imagine doing them – is it joyful or stressed? And then we ask:

- Is the action something that fits my values, my understanding of good?
- Is it a gift that I'm ready to experience and express?
- Does doing this act of service feel Effortless, Enjoyable, Energizing?
- Is my "cup overflowing" so this action will not leave me drained?

If all of these answers are "yes," it's probably an act of service that all involved will benefit from. If any of them are "no" then it's likely that your effort will cost you something and have less than the desired effect on anyone else involved. Or it may simply be that now is not the time.

In most cases, our most effective service comes from inspirations we receive in the Silence. And there's no sense of sacrifice or effort involved. We simply follow our natural inclinations to use our gifts and talents, and the world is a better place! We show up where we feel "called" by some inner voice to be, ready to experience and express our true nature, trusting that something wonderful is unfolding—and it does!

If you're having trouble believing all this, think of the most powerfully effective experiences you ever had—the times you've created or been part of something that really felt good, deeply satisfying. Now consider the impact that activity had on yourself and others.

Chances are, whether it was a party or a yearbook or a production or an election campaign, it was Enjoyable (fun, lots of pleasant moments), Effortless (you could hardly wait to get to it, didn't have to struggle at all, even if it was challenging and you pushed your limits), and, though you may have been physically tired, you truly felt great (Energized)!

Service is *always* a mutually beneficial experience—"enlightened self-interest." And in spite of what many of us were taught, if it's not, it's not truly service.

Afterword

That's it! Four simple practices: the "4 Ss in Spiritual Success." That's all it takes to maintain a healthy spiritual life, to maintain the energy and enthusiasm and ongoing capacity we need to respond to the shifts and changes of human existence—to begin to make that wonderful sense of divine connection our regular, everyday experience..

So, as you develop your own daily practice, simply remember to include:

- **Study**—a few minutes to an hour each day immersed in inspiring ideas and words;
- **Silence**—at least once, and ideally twice a day for 15-50

minutes, simply focusing on something other than your normal thought patterns, open to experiencing new insights;

- **Sharing**—an hour or so several times each week with others who are on a similar path, exploring similar ideas and experiences;
- **Service**—expressing your gifts and talents in ways that are Effortless, Enjoyable, and Energizing, for the betterment of the folks around you.

Research (and the author's own experience) has shown that, when we do these 4 simple things several times a week, we are physically healthier, mentally clearer, socially more comfortable, and much more effective in all that we undertake.

It's worth it. Really. A few minutes to an hour several times a week can make all the difference in our ability to cope with life in this world.

So go ahead! Give it a try! And, above all, enjoy!

rlm

About the Author:

Ruth L. Miller, Ph.D., is a cultural cybernetician and New Thought minister with multiple degrees and decades of experience researching the nature of consciousness and culture. She lives, writes, counsels, and teaches in the Pacific Northwestern United States.

For more information about her work or her books, go to her website: www.ruthlmillerphd.com.